How Does My Home Work?
Water

Chris Oxlade

Heinemann
LIBRARY

Chicago, Illinois

www.capstonepub.com

Visit our website to find out more information about Heinemann-Raintree books.

To order:

☎ Phone 800-747-4992

💻 Visit www.capstonepub.com to browse our catalog and order online.

Edited by Daniel Nunn, Rebecca Rissman,
  and Catherine Veitch
Designed by Joanna Hinton-Malivoire
Picture research by Elizabeth Alexander
Production by Alison Parsons
Originated by Capstone Global Library Ltd
Printed and bound in China by Leo Paper Products

16 15 14 13 12
10 9 8 7 6 5 4 3 2 1

Library of Congress Cataloging-in-Publication Data
Oxlade, Chris.
  Water / Chris Oxlade.—1st ed.
    p. cm.—(How does my home work?)
  Includes bibliographical references and index.
  ISBN 978-1-4329-6567-9 (hb)—ISBN 978-1-4329-6572-3 (pb)
  1. Water—Juvenile literature. I. Title.
  GB662.3.O954 2013
  363.6'1—dc23   2011038250

Acknowledgments
We would like to thank the following for permission to reproduce photographs: Corbis p. 11 (© Mike Kemp/Tetra Images); Dreamstime.com pp. 18 (© Bartlomiej Jaworski), 23 (© Bartlomiej Jaworski); Getty Images p. 9 (Dorling Kindersley); iStockphoto pp. 4 (© Yarinca), 7 (© Alan Lagadu), 8 (© asterix0597), 10 (© Nicolas Loran), 21 (© David Cannings-Bushell), 23 (© Alan Lagadu), 23 (© David Cannings-Bushell); Photolibrary p. 19 (Paul Glendell/Still Pictures); Shutterstock pp. 5 (© Ami Parikh), 6 (© Dmitry Naumov), 12 (© Vetal), 13 (© Wade H. Massie), 14 (© Romanenkova), 15 (© dusan964), 16 (© Nomad_Soul), 20 (© Max Topchii), 23 (© Elena Ray), 23 (© Richard Thornton), 23 (© Romanenkova), 23 (© Nomad_Soul).

Cover photograph of washing hands reproduced with permission of Shutterstock (© g215). Background photograph of underwater bubbles reproduced with permission of Shutterstock (© George Toubalis).

Back cover photographs of (left) a dam reproduced with permission of iStockphoto (© Alan Lagadu), and (right) a faucet reproduced with permission of iStockphoto (© Nicolas Loran).

Every effort has been made to contact copyright holders of material reproduced in this book. Any omissions will be rectified in subsequent printings if notice is given to the publisher.

We would like to thank Darren Horn for his invaluable help in the preparation of this book.

Disclaimer
All the Internet addresses (URLs) given in this book were valid at the time of going to press. However, due to the dynamic nature of the Internet, some addresses may have changed, or sites may have changed or ceased to exist since publication. While the author and Publishers regret any inconvenience this may cause readers, no responsibility for any such changes can be accepted by either the author or the Publishers.

Contents

Some words are shown in bold, **like this**. You can find them in the glossary on page 23.

Why Do We Need Water?

At home we need water for drinking and for cooking.

You have to drink water every day to stay healthy.

In the garden, we give water to plants to help them grow.

We also need water for washing ourselves and our clothes.

Where Do We Get Water?

We get most of our water from rain.

When rain falls, some of the rain flows into streams and rivers.

dam

We store water from rivers in lakes called **reservoirs**.

A **dam** stops the water from flowing away.

How Does Water Get to My Home?

pipe

Water travels to your home along pipes.

Giant pipes carry the water from **reservoirs** to towns and cities.

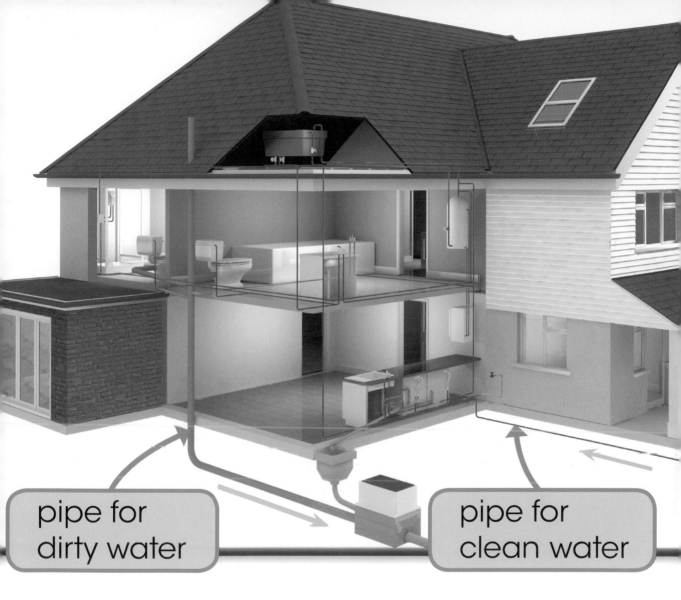

pipe for
dirty water

pipe for
clean water

The giant pipes carry water under the
ground along the streets.

Narrow pipes take the water from the giant
pipes into homes.

Why Does Water Come Out of a Faucet?

Powerful **pumps** push the water along the pipes to your home.

When you open a faucet, this push makes water flow out of the faucet.

leak

Sometimes a water pipe gets a leak.

This can happen if water in the pipe freezes into ice and splits the pipe.

Dirty water from your home goes down special pipes called drains.

The drains from each home join big underground pipes called **sewers**.

12

Sewers carry the dirty water to a **water treatment plant** to clean it.

The cleaned water then goes into a river or to the sea.

Why Does Dirty Water Need to Be Cleaned?

Dirty water is dangerous to drink or to swim in.

If a person drinks or swallows dirty water, he or she can become very ill.

dead fish

Dirty water often has harmful chemicals in it.

The chemicals can harm the animals and plants that live in rivers and oceans.

How Much Water Do We Use at Home?

A washing machine uses about 25 **gallons** of water for each load of washing.

That is enough to fill up your bathtub!

Activity	Amount of Water
Taking a shower	8 gallons
Taking a bath	25 gallons
One toilet flush	1 ½ gallons
Washing machine load	25 gallons
Running the faucet	2 ½ gallons a minute

This table shows how much water we use for different things.

Each day, a person uses between 26 and 52 gallons of water at home.

Can We Use as Much Water as We Want?

reservoir

When the weather is very dry, the amount of water in **reservoirs** goes down.

Then we need to be even more careful not to use more water than we need.

Sometimes, an underground pipe bursts and no water comes out of your faucets.

Then water has to be brought to your street in water trucks.

How Can We Use Less Water?

You can use less water in many ways.

One way to save water is to turn the faucet off while you brush your teeth.

rain barrel

A **rain barrel** collects rainwater that flows off your home's roof.

You can use this water to water plants or clean your car, instead of tap water.

21

Keep a Water Diary

Copy this table onto a sheet of paper.

Make a tally of how many times your family uses water in one day. Do you think you could have saved any water?

Activity	Gallons of Water	Tally
Toilet flush	1 ½	卌 |||
Shower	8	|||
Bath	25	||
Washing machine	25		
Dishwasher	15		
Running a faucet	2 ½ (each minute)	卌 卌

Glossary

 **dam** thick wall that holds water in a reservoir

 **gallon** measure of the space that some liquid takes up. A large jug of milk is one gallon.

 **pump** machine that pushes water from one place to another

 **rain barrel** large barrel used for catching and keeping rainwater

 **reservoir** large body of water that holds water for homes

 **sewer** large pipe for carrying away dirty water and waste from drains

 **water treatment plant** place where dirty water is cleaned

Find Out More

Books

Fix, Alexandra. *Reduce, Reuse, Recycle: Water*. Chicago: Heinemann Library, 2008.

Guillain, Charlotte. *Help the Environment: Saving Water*. Chicago: Heinemann Library, 2008.

Website

www.epa.gov/students/games.html
Play fun and educational games on this website. Click around to learn more about how you can help the environment.

Index